The Totally Geeky Guide to

P THE RINCESS BRIDE

The Totally Geeky Guide to

THE PRINCESS BRIDE

by MaryAnn Johanson

First edition August 2006

ISBN: 978-1-84728-739-7

Contact the author:
MaryAnn Johanson
PO Box 221
Bronx, NY 10470

thechick@flickfilosopher.com

More cinematic observations and geeky thinkery by MaryAnn Johanson:
flickfilosopher.com
geekphilosophy.com
cinemarati.org

for everyone who has ever wondered
why murder by pirates is good

CONTENTS

INTRODUCTION

The Princess Bride has always been with me. I don't remember the first time I saw the film, though I'm pretty sure I did not see it during its theatrical release and only stumbled across it on video. But I can't remember a time before *The Princess Bride*, a time in which I did not have its wit and snark to guide me through life in all its pain. And I can say that life is pain with a smile, nay, a happy-go-lucky grin, because the Man in Black said so right here in this silly, wonderful, perfectly perfect movie. I mean, it's got everything: fencing, fighting, torture, revenge, giants, monsters, chases, escapes, true love, miracles—

But you knew that, didn't you, and you know, if you're like me, that I could happily babble on for hours uttering nothing but lines of dialogue from *The Princess Bride*. If you're not sure if you're like me, if you're not sure if this book is for you, then simply take this easy quiz:

Are you a *Princess Bride* fanatic?

Who is the sworn enemy of the country of Florin?
A. Rosencranz
B. Guildenstern
C. Guilder

Name the fencing strategy to counter Bonetti's Defense.
A. Casablanca
B. Copernicus
C. Capoferro

Finish this sentence: Plato, Aristotle, and Socrates are...
A. Morons
B. Dead
C. Philosophers

Where was Fezzik the Giant unemployed when Vizzini hired him?
A. Greenland
B. The WWF
C. Hollywood

To avoid the first Classic Blunder, you should:

A. Never go up against a Sicilian when death is on the line.

B. Never get involved in a land war in Asia.

C. Never utter a line from *The Princess Bride* unless you want to be spouting quotes all day.

The Princess Bride was written by:

A. William Goldman

B. S. Morgenstern

C. This is a trick question, isn't it?

Is this a kissing book?

A. Yes

B. No

C. You know, someday you might not mind so much.

ANSWERS

Well, if you don't know, I'm not going to spoil the movie for you by giving away all the fun. But if you're thinking, "Hey, why not ask what the three terrors of the Fire Swamp are, or why no one would surrender to the Dread Pirate Westley, or what 'as you wish' means, or what interpersonal institution is considered 'a dweam within a dweam?'" then you already know what kind of fanatic you are. Read on.

I

"I'M ONLY WAITING AROUND TO KILL YOU..."

It's not as if it's something you do deliberately. No one thinks to herself, "Ah, now's my chance to test my new pal on his knowledge of *The Princess Bride*." It just happens naturally. You're wishing each other farewell and you say, "Have fun storming the castle!" Or you're discussing the idiocy of a third party and you say, "That's one of the classic blunders," or perhaps, as if to scold that idiot blunderer: "You keep using that word. I don't think it means what you think it means."

And then it happens. Your new pal screws up his face in a mystified grimace—he has no idea what you're talking about. And you, hoping to salvage the situation, prompt him: "You know, *The Princess Bride*? Inconceivable? Hello, my name is Inigo Montoya? No?"

There are only three possible outcomes at this point. One, your friend says, "Oh, I've never seen that." Which is sad, but it means there's still some hope for him, and you will have the opportunity to initiate a neophyte into the cinematic equivalent of a not-so-secret secret society. Two, your friend says, "Oh, that. I think I saw that once." Which is bad, because there's no such thing as seeing *The Princess Bride* "once"—if you haven't seen it so many times that you unconsciously mouth the dialogue along with the action, you haven't really seen it at all. Three, your friend says, "Oh, that. I never really got that movie." Which is the point at which you stop calling him friend.

Extreme? Perhaps. But all true worshippers at the altar of the Dread Pirate Westley have done it, have looked askance at someone we thought we knew who suddenly shows himself to be an alien creature beyond our ken. Not having seen *The Princess Bride* is almost understandable, but not getting it? That indicates a discordance between you and this so-called friend on a level so fundamental that it cannot be overcome. What do you say to someone who isn't tickled by the concept that being murdered by pirates can be good? How can you ever look such a person in the eye again? Someone I used to know, someone whom I liked and

The simple truth is that *The Princess Bride* is one of those films that caught me at a pivotal moment in my moviegoing life, when watching something infused with the sheer bliss of fantasy made it easy to love what movies could offer. It became second only to Monty Python and that other early Rob Reiner film, *This Is Spinal Tap*, among my cohort group as quote fodder.
—Scott Renshaw, film critic and entertainment editor,
Salt Lake City Weekly

respected, suddenly told me one day that she thought *The Princess Bride* was "dumb." I was devastated, not that she had insulted my movie but that I could never see her as quite the same sharp cookie I had before. She had, in my eyes, insulted only herself.

I'm only half kidding. There is a kinship among people who "get" *The Princess Bride* that isn't about the movie per se but about sharing a particular outlook on the world, one that does not tolerate bullshit, mundanity, or obviousness. People who "get" *The Princess Bride* "get" irony and sarcasm. People who "get" *The Princess Bride* do not suffer fools gladly. People who "get" *The Princess Bride* long for swashbuckling romantic adventure while simultaneously acknowledging the impossibility of such a dream. To be a *Princess Bride* fan is more than to be in the grip of mere "fannishness." It is to be possessed of a deep and abiding feeling that all knowledge and wisdom is to be found in *The Princess Bride.* It is to be convinced that there is no single moment of human experience for which there is not an appropriate quote from the film... and it is have those quotes spring to mind of their own accord in the course of everyday life. And it is to realize that, as extraordinary and hilarious and perfect as the film is, it is still, in the end, only a movie.

People who "get" *The Princess Bride* are of that special breed of cynics who are thwarted idealists. Of course there are people who don't "get" *The Princess Bride* who aren't reluctant cynics, who don't yearn for adventure, who don't, in fact, sense that the wisdom of humanity is contained within its frames. But it's impossible to imagine someone who does feel all these things not "getting" *The Princess Bride*... and the corollary, then, is that anyone who "gets" *The Princess Bride* is almost certain to share all those qualities and characteristics. Love and appreciation for the movie becomes shorthand for an almost guaranteed simpatico.

There's never anything malicious or conniving in The *Princess Bride* Test, because drawing upon the movie for commentary on life, the universe, and everything is reflexive, almost unconscious on the part of any fan of the film. The movie's philosophy is so attuned to our own that quoting from it is totally natural; in fact, we only ever realize we're testing a new acquaintance when he or she fails the Test, when his or her response reminds us that it is not normal and natural to lament the reality that there's not a lot of money in revenge; that most people, if they even bothered to think about such things, would consider the lack of remuneration involved in the revenge business quite obvious.

Obvious, yes, but not the kind of clichéd Hollywood obvious that *Princess Bride* fans want nothing to do with. It's a questioning-reality kind of obvious, an über obvious that refuses to take anything for granted, an all-seeing obvious that points out the strings tugging at the puppet theater of the world. *Bride* holds up for gentle ridicule the pretense of movies as well as our own eagerness to be fooled by them; it pokes at the relationship between storyteller and audience in order to unravel the mystery of why we give ourselves over to fantasy; it celebrates the joy of story while it simultaneously pulls out the supports that hold up fiction.

There's a word for people who not only appreciate but seek out mere entertainments that undermine social and cultural preconceptions. There's a word for people who think about things that most people take so much for granted that they don't even realize they're not thinking about them. And that word is "geek."

II

"You keep using that word..."

Film geek. Fantasy geek. Fencing geek. One of those terms likely applies to you. Whatever draws you to *The Princess Bride*, chances are it's operating on a high level of pleasant, recreational obsessiveness—you're consumed by the escapism of movies; you're in love with fanciful stories about pseudomedieval realms; you know every fencing move, own your own épée, and can't believe that all movies don't get swordplay this perfectly perfect; maybe all of the above. That's fine, and quite normal— there is no need to see a doctor; mind-pacifying pharmaceuticals are not called for. But I know that you were moved to pick up this book in a kind of fit of self-deprecating, ironically detached desperation, frantic to figure out just why this wonderful, glorious, silly film has such a hold over you. And I know this because 1) If you don't already have a self-deprecating, ironically detached sense of humor, you wouldn't be in the thrall of *The Princess Bride*, and 2) People who aren't obsessed with movies, for whatever reason, do not read self-deprecating, ironically detached but hopefully humorous book-length essays about them.

Look, you're a geek. It's okay. Take a deep breath.

Geek. Say it out loud: Geek.

Some people, even those who would call themselves geeks, consider it a dirty word. Others consider it derogatory. It should be neither. "Geek" is the new "intellectual," only a whole lot less stuffy, and a whole lot more fun: geeks apply the thinkyness of intellectualism to pop culture, and we're making smarts cool while we're also redeeming our own love of the objects of our obsessions. Geeks are no mere passive watchers of television or thoughtless consumers of film. Geeks are active participants in pop culture, absorbing it, analyzing it, regurgitating it as commentary on the larger culture.

And there couldn't be a better example of the conectedness with and engaged relationship to pop culture than the cult of *The Princess Bride.* The cult of *The Princess Bride* may well have been, in retrospect, inevitable... particularly since it came along at precisely the right time to take advantage of a new technology that was about to change the movie industry—and movie fandom—forever.

See, test screenings prior to the film's release had shown that college kids were likely to be its biggest audience, but poor marketing ensured that they never got the word that this was a movie not to miss. And so, when the film opened in the United States on nine screens in September 1987 after a few film festival screenings worldwide, it enjoyed only modest box office and critical success. The first real following for *Bride* was built—slowly but certainly—on the word of mouth that spread as the film's key audience finally caught up with it after its VHS release.

And the VCR had only just arrived as a must-have home-entertainment gadget—by 1988, 60 percent of U.S. households had at least one. Geek culture would never have developed as it has without the VCR. When you can view movies and television shows multiple times on any schedule, it qualitatively changes how you react to them: You feel their rhythms more acutely when numerous viewings invariably lead to memorization of its dialogue; you almost can't help but begin to think about the characters and motifs and themes in a more profound way. *The Princess Bride* wouldn't be the touchstone that it is without this new way of not just viewing but absorbing movies.

Video, and now DVD, allows *Bride*—and all movies that have engendered devoted followings—to be approached less like a transitory experience that washes over you and then is finished, and more like a work of literature that can be examined and considered from all angles. You can put down a book and ponder what you've read so far before you continue. You can jump back to earlier chapters in a book and clarify some point of plot or character. You can reread your favorite bits in a book out of order, or even jump to the finale (if you must) and find out how it all ends. And with home video, we lovers of film could do all this with a movie.

But if there was suddenly new technology available that allowed viewers to dissect and deconstruct pop culture, that did not automatically mean that every film was worth dissecting and deconstructing. Why *The Princess Bride*? Why not, say, the Kevin

Costner thriller *No Way Out,* which was released a month before *Bride* and pulled in about the same amount of cash at the box office, indicating a similar degree of approval from the moviegoing audience? What aspects of the film make it so cult-lovable in the first place?

It starts, I think, with a golden age...

III

"I WAS ELEVEN YEARS OLD…"

S cience fiction editor and critic David Hartwell has said that he believes that the golden age of science fiction is not the 1930s or the 1950s but… 12. The best or most successful or most worthy works of the fantastic, he suggests, are not the products of a particular decade or of a certain literary movement but those we read at the moment when our sense of wonder is at a peak; the imagination is captured more by our state of mind than as a result of the supposed classicness of what we're reading.

Now, most people you'll meet who profess to *Princess Bride* worship will likely have been somewhat older than 12 when they first saw the film—I certainly was in my 20s before I caught up with it. It's true, though, that many of those who are drawn to *Bride,* regardless of when they first experienced it, will have had their little minds warped at that vulnerable pubescent moment, the impact of which is lifelong. You never really stop being drawn to this kind of stuff once you're in its thrall. But for those who failed to have that transcendent childhood experience, there's an element of the film that allows anyone, no matter how old, to become a kid again at the precise critical age that will allow the movie to rocket its way directly to the imagination center of the brain. And that is the framing story around the faux medieval adventure, of the modern grandfather (played by Peter Falk) reading the "good parts" version of "S. Morgenstern"'s "classic" "novel" *The Princess Bride* to his grandson (played by Fred Savage).

The Grandson's situation alone is enough to slam anyone who grew up in America in the second half of the twentieth century right back to powerless childhood—Savage, in the retrospective documentary "As You Wish" on the Special Edition DVD of the film, describes his characters as an "everykid," and he is. His plight is one that we all appreciate with a groan of recognition: he's stuck in bed, too sick to go to school or outside to play but not so sick

We identify first not with Westley or Buttercup, but with the boy in bed—stepping back into childhood, that time when disbelief was easier to suspend—and so are seduced by the story, drawn into the intrigue and adventure, with an imagination automatically prepared to accept the "Cliffs of Insanity" as a real place—even as our "knowing" adult self smiles at the irony.
—Stephen Gerringer,
Campbellian folklorist and "Practical Campbell"
columnist for the Joseph Campbell Foundation [jcf.org],
in an interview with the author

that he doesn't need diversion. He's well enough to be bored, and the video baseball game he's playing isn't doing it: the inelegant game may have been the state of the art when the film was made, and hence the height of possible distraction for the Grandson, but today, two decades later, its clunkiness only serves as an even more potent reminder that high-tech toys are no substitute for deceptively simple storytelling.

Not that the Grandson realizes this at first; his resistance to being read to—from a *book*—and his gradual giving of himself over to the power of the written word is more than mere humor recalling our own childhood reluctance to sample new experiences... though that is indeed even funnier from the perspective of comparatively more sophisticated adulthood, which knows that many of the things we once found icky and boring and stupid are now some of the best things life has to offer.

But that's also a perfect metaphor for the resistance some moviegoers might feel toward quote-unquote fantasy if they weren't fortunate enough to be exposed to such things at the proper age. Rodents of Unusual Size and Miracle Pills and the like—there are, I've heard tell, otherwise perfectly pleasant people who are unable to buy the reality of such things, and so avoid movies about them. And the conceit that we are being read to—for we are, too, along with the Grandson—is a way to overcome such reluctance to trust to imagination.

Where other films typically posit even the most absurd things as "real" (within the world of the film)—and ask us to accept without question invading aliens, tiny hobbits, whatever—here the whole medieval fantasy story and all its attendant absurdities are self-consciously fake, are "only" a story. The structure of the film adds a level of remove that invites—even demands—that we not "believe" a word of it... or believe as much or as little as we care to.

The Grandson? He has no tolerance for the "kissing" stuff, as the Grandfather begins to read, and his disdain shapes our anticipation of what we're about to see: we join the Grandson in poo-pooing the romance (at least at first) and demand action, excitement, swordfighting, murder by pirates! It apes the approach many moviegoers—particularly the young and impatient audience that action/adventure films are typically aimed at—take to watching movies: We don't want to watch the slow setting-up stuff that lots of movies feel the need to throw at us before things starts blowing up (metaphorically, in the case of *Bride*), we want to get right to the good stuff! What happens as a result is that *Bride* is as much about how we watch movies as it is a movie itself.

IV

"SHE DOESN'T GET EATEN BY THE EELS AT THIS TIME..."

You almost cannot talk about *The Princess Bride* without winking. The whole thing is a giant put-on... which all movies are, of course. The difference is that this film is constantly reminding us that it's all a sham, a fake. Usually, that's something you want to forget—the viewer wants to get lost in a film, not be told that it's a joke at our expense. But in making us very consciously aware of the mechanisms by which movies entertain us, *Bride* ends up entertaining us even more, surprising us in a way that few movies even dare attempt.

It's like this. The ironic quotation marks I used before—"classic," "novel," etc.—were demanded because, as all true fans of the film know, "S. Morgenstern's *The Princess Bride*" is an invention of screenwriter William Goldman. This conceit, though, of the film being a "good parts" abridgement of a novel you've never heard is so powerfully effective that a casual fan of the film—if such a creature exists—would be forgiven for thinking the book really does exist... that is, that S. Morgenstern was a genuine novelist from a real country called Florin who wrote an actual book called *The Princess Bride* that William Goldman did, in fact, abridge and which was then adapted for film. Which is not the case at all: Goldman wrote the novel that purports to be an abridgement of Morgenstern, it was published in 1973, and no book version of *The Princess Bride* exists except Goldman's. Hell, I know that, but I would swear to the Impressive Clergyman that I once walked into a used-book store in a little fishing village on Long Island and saw there on a dusty shelf a vintage copy of the Morgenstern novel. Why I didn't buy it, I can't say, except that this entire experience must have been a figment of my iocane-addled brain. There is no other explanation.

Or is there? Maybe the Morgenstern does exist, and Goldman has pulled a triple-cross on us, convincing us to buy the book as real in that suspension-of-disbelief way we approach movies, but then saying, "Oh no, it's just a joke," all the while secretly holding this actual, old, out-of-print and impossible-to-find novel in reserve to be revealed upon his death, or something equally dramatic. I don't really believe this, of course—it's all Goldman's lark. Or is it? It would certainly match the delicious tricksiness of the film that was adapted from Goldman's novel, a film that plays with the conventions not just of filmmaking but of storytelling itself, undercutting the kind of suspense we expect from movies, undercutting the very necessity of the suspension of disbelief required to appreciate and enjoy almost any story. It seems contradictory to say that perhaps one of the most beloved films of the last twenty years—if not in the whole century-plus of film—succeeds partly because it does precisely what a movie should not do: constantly nudges us, inviting us to laugh along with it, in love with its own jape. The movie can't help snickering at its own cleverness, and inviting us to snicker too.

Goldman is constantly reminding us though his script that what we are watching is a Movie... and he never lets us forget that we are consumers of a product designed to elicit certain reactions in us. When, for instance, Princess Buttercup is in great danger, seemingly, of being eaten by the Shrieking Eels, the logical part of our moviegoing brains knows that she will be fine, she'll be safe—she has to be safe, because she is a major character in this story, and her story has not yet resolved itself in any way that satisfies what we unconsciously understand are the demands of storytelling: she must be reunited with Westley, her true love, or she must fail to be reunited with him through some action or fault of her own: dumb circumstance may rule real life, but it violates the conventions of effective storytelling. If we cannot take some lesson from Buttercup's travails to apply to our own lives, there is no point to her tale, and we simply don't know enough about her yet to draw any conclusions from her story. There would be no reason for her story to exist if it ended here.

So we know she is fine; her safety is absolutely assured. But we're supposed to pretend we don't know—it's part of the unspoken contract between storyteller and audience: if the storyteller ensures that his story is gripping enough, the audience will play along. The real trick is this: When the storyteller is very good, the audience doesn't even know it's playing along: the audience fools itself into thinking it feels genuine suspense. And that's what happens with the Shrieking Eels: anticipation of an attack and anxiety over Buttercup's fate builds in such a way that we forget to remember that we have no reason to worry about her safety...

And then it's all simply sliced away by the Grandfather/narrator's line "She doesn't get eaten by the eels at this time." It's an involuntary laugh that most viewers bark out at this point, even after the fiftieth viewing: Movies just aren't supposed to do this. Movies aren't supposed to subvert their own potency this way. We were—like the Grandson, scrunching up his bedsheets in his fists in a paroxysm of tension—actually tense, afraid for Buttercup, because the emotional power of the moment trumps any sense of the logical that tells us not to worry, and our laugh is like the Grandson's astonished "What?!"

In a movie full of uniquely memorable elements (exciting duels, a rhyming giant, the Pit of Despair, Cliffs of Insanity, and more), this single line—"She doesn't get eaten by the eels at this time"—may be the one that defines the curious appeal of *The Princess Bride*. In "As You Wish," director Rob Reiner calls his film "a celebration of storytelling"... but the truly odd thing is that

> I thought the movie was going to be fabulous and wonderful and very popular. I thought it was going to be a big hit. And oddly enough, it wasn't when it first came out, because I think the studio didn't really know how to market it. They didn't know to market it as a romance, a romantic comedy, a comedy, or an adventure, and the fact is that it's all of those things.
> **—actor Chris Sarandon, aka "Prince Humperdinck," in an interview with the author**

the film celebrates storytelling by deliberately and with comic aforethought pointing out how artificial storytelling is—and yet, at the same time, it is so effective an example of storytelling that even constant reminders that what we are being presented is fake cannot undermine it. If *Bride* celebrates anything, it is our supreme willingness to be fooled in the name of entertainment, our deep desire to give ourselves over to the fantasy of fiction.

Bride is full of bits like this one, bits that defy the very essence of effective storytelling, bits that tweak the metaphoric nose of audience expectations. But because this scene embodies the very spirit of *Bride*'s weirdness and humor, it's no wonder that it is the line "She doesn't get eaten by the eels at this time" and the Grandson's shocked response that prompts Reiner, in his commentary on the Special Edition DVD, to say:

> *People said, "You can't break away from the film like this. People will lose the thread of the story. They won't be able to get reinvolved." I said, "No, I think it's just gonna make people get more involved."...*

It's easy to see how such a sharp divergence from what audiences anticipate from a film could prompt nervous jitters among studio executives (who are undoubtedly the "people" Reiner is referring to)—not only because execs fear that audiences really will be turned off by something too bizarre but because studios simply don't know how to market films that defy expectations. The marketing of a film is all about setting up expectations and then fulfilling those expectations, about offering hints about which particular storytelling tropes will be trotted out in the film's story.

Bride trots out tropes, sure... but then it smashes them. (Watch the original theatrical trailer for *Bride*—it's on the DVD. It's confused and confusing, and whoever cut it clearly hasn't the foggiest idea what the formula is for selling a movie about undercutting movie formulas. It may be the single worst trailer in the history of cinema.)

Screenwriter William Goldman, in his commentary on the Special Edition DVD, notes ironically that because the film managed to overcome its poor marketing to become such a cult favorite today, now all he hears from Hollywood powers that be is "I want something like *Princess Bride.*" That we very rarely ever see something that even approaches the triumph of *Bride* is a testament to how very difficult it is to create a story that can overcome our skepticism, even as eager as we are to be fooled by a pretense and fakery. It must be said again: that *Bride* manages this even while never ceasing to hit us about the head with its own falseness is astonishing. It's part of why the movie never fails to tickle, even upon the umpteenth viewing: because our sense of what's right and appropriate and proper in the structure of a story never changes—it's almost as if we forget to remember that the Grandfather is going to undercut the suspense we were enjoying over Buttercup's fate.

And there's more irony yet, for us *Bride* fans. While we forget to remember everything we know about cinematic storytelling while watching *Bride,* our love of *Bride*'s clever self-awareness has ruined us for lots of other, less obviously self-aware films.

"He is a sailor on the pirate ship Revenge..."

It is a fundamental fact of the universe that there is no film quite like *The Princess Bride*. But that's a cheap way of dealing with the age-old conundrum of the movie fan: "If I like *Movie X*, what other movies should I be watching?"

The easy answer here is, of course, encompasses the slew of films that could be loosely defined as "fractured fairy tales" and were very likely inspired, at least in some small part, by *The Princess Bride*. Recent entries in this fantasy subgenre include *Shrek* (2001), *Shrek 2* (2004), *Chicken Little* (2005), and *Hoodwinked* (2006), all of which fricassée archetypes, upend mythologies, and ask us to take a fresh look at stories and characters we thought we knew. If you prefer live-action humans skewering old tales, check out *Ever After* (1998), a feminist recasting of *Cinderella*; it's less raucous than *Bride* but still cheeky and charming. *Ella Enchanted* (2004) eschews animation, too, but unfortunately also omits wit, enchantment, and grace; this sendup of the tropes of medieval fantasy is about as buoyant as a lead balloon, but it's worth a viewing by *Bride* fans for the appearance by Cary Elwes in a decidedly un-Westley-esque role as a cartoonishly evil nobleman.

Less funny but a whole lot more fun—and a whole lot closer in spirit to *The Princess Bride*—are the classic adventure dramas that clearly served as instigations for *Bride* screenwriter William Goldman and director Rob Reiner. In the retrospective documentary "As You Wish," which appears on the Special Edition *Princess Bride* DVD, Reiner comments that Cary Elwes strongly resembles, at least as Westley, actor Douglas Fairbanks Jr.—and Reiner is right. But in fact, it is the films of Fairbanks' father, Douglas Fairbanks Sr., that are the most distant ancestors of *Bride*. In the 1920s, the elder Fairbanks starred in a series of silent, black-and-white adventure films—the original action movies—with such enticing titles as *The Mark of Zorro* (1920), *The Three Musketeers* (1921), *Robin Hood* (1922), *The Thief of Bagdad* (1924), *The Black Pirate* (1926), and *Iron Mask* (1929). All are available on DVD.

The Fairbanks films may appeal more to serious cineastes and buffs of cinematic history than to those just looking for a good time at the movies. But that's exactly what's on offer in the Golden Age swashbucklers starring Errol Flynn, a direct descendent of Fairbanks' adventurer and an immediate forerunner of Elwes's Man in Black... and not just because Westley is an expert swordsman, revels in derring-do, and sports a rakish moustache. Westley's journey from innocent farmboy to brigand and man of the world is echoed by the increasing sophistication of Flynn's characters over the course of three films: In *Captain Blood* (1935), he is Dr. Peter Blood, a good man but something of a homebody who is forced by a travesty of justice and exigent circumstance into a life of piracy; then, in *The Adventures of Robin Hood* (1938), Flynn is a medieval aristocrat compelled by his own sense of integrity to become a rebel for righteousness; and finally, in *The Sea Hawk* (1940), he is Captain Geoffrey Thorpe, a privateer, an agent on the high seas for Her Majesty Queen Elizabeth I, a criminal with official sanction but an honest and honorable fellow nevertheless.

There are moments of humor in all three films, though they're nowhere near being all-out comedies... but my guess is that most fans of *The Princess Bride* would not name the humor as the aspect of the movie that is fundamentally the most engaging. Witty quotability aside, there is a palpable sense of intrepid voyaging and exciting discovery to *Bride*, one that any hotblooded movie fan yearns to experience for oneself: Who wouldn't love to scale the Cliffs of Insanity, or be serenaded in the moonlight by the Shrieking Eels (from the safety of a ship, of course), or pop into the Thieves' Forest to share a mug of ale in a seedy pub with a gang of cutthroats and pickpockets? That feeling—that life was once more exciting, more dangerous, more alive— makes for part of *Bride*'s witty quotability: "I've hired you to help me start a war. It's an prestigious line of work, with a long and glorious tradition." And this is what the Flynn movies are all about: everything from the star's passionate performances to director Michael Curtiz's energetic flair for intense action will thrill *Bride* fans looking for more of the same. (After these three classics, Curtiz would go on to make another film that has moved generations of moviegoers with its depiction of noble causes and true love: *Casablanca*.)

Oh, for sure, there're lots of amusing analogs to be found between *Bride* and the Flynn films, too—you can almost make a game of it. Observe how Claude Rains' evil Prince John in *Robin Hood* looks incredibly like Christopher Guest's Count Rugen; I'd be shocked, shocked to learn that *Bride*'s costume designers had not taken style cues from bad Prince John. Discern how the Man in Black's initial encounters with Fezzik and Inigo resonate with a frisson of Robin's contests, in that same film, with Little John and Friar Tuck. You'll enjoy extra piratey goodness in *Captain Blood* when you recognize what a direct and obvious influence it was on the modern film that most closely reverberates with *Bride*'s drollery, intelligence, and jauntiness: 2003's *Pirates of the Caribbean: The Curse of the Black Pearl*.

A final note: In your explorations of classic *Bride*-ish films, you may come across the intriguingly named *The Princess and the Pirate,* from 1944. If *Bride* is Monty Python–esque, then this goofy lark comes via the Marx Brothers, and while it is indeed a cinematic hoot, it bears little resemblance to our beloved film. It sounds, on the surface, as if it might: Virginia Mayo plays a princess who's running away to marry her true love, instead of the man her father the king has lined up for her, and along the way she's kidnapped by pirates who hold her for ransom. Her rescuer, though, is Bob Hope, portraying a vaudeville performer long before vaudeville was ever invented, which is far from the only hilarious anachronism the film indulges in: Hope's stage clown is meta-aware that he's in a movie and is constantly winking at the audience and nudging us in reminder. Modern and ironic it is—in the vein of *The Princess Bride* it isn't. ●

V

"Have Fun Storming the Castle?"

Admit it: you've done this. You're watching a movie, something very dramatic, perhaps, intense and exciting, with violent shootouts and passionate, dedicated cops chasing conflicted, tormented mafiosos, and it's all very earnest and serious and important and the whole cast are Method actors who all rushed to the seclusion of rehab when they finished shooting, they were so torn up by the experience. This one is definitely headed for the Oscars, it is absolutely destined to become a golden cinematic legend. It's damn good stuff, and you're really caught up in it, sitting right on the edge of your seat, your popcorn cast aside, forgotten— your stomach is too twisted up to possibly eat anything.

Then it happens. The angst-ridden police detective is gut-shot in the middle of a garbage-strewn urban street, eliciting a collective gasp of shock from the audience, and while his lifeblood gurgles out onto the pavement—and grim music swells on the score, and the black-and-white film stock somehow gets even grainer than it has been—he whispers a hoarse apology to his wise old veteran partner, sorry about how he let them all down. He expires right there in the gutter without ever revealing to anyone else the vital clue that will bring down the bad guys, and how will justice be done and order be restored and wrongs be righted now?

And you know it with a sudden certainty, and you can't help it, you really can't, you try to suck it in and keep quiet and not ruin the film for anyone else but you're going to explode if you don't say it. So you lean to the friend next to you and whisper in the movie-theater darkness: "I bet he's only mostly dead." And because you could only feel so unignorable a compulsion to say such a thing in the presence of someone who has passed The *Princess Bride* Test, your friend, no matter how engrossed by the film he was too, will invariably let out a snort of laughter and probably respond with a simple "Look who knows so much" or perhaps put a contextually appropriate spin on it: "This is a noble cause. His police chief is corrupt. His enemies are on the brink of victory..."

Is *The Princess Bride* the most quotable movie ever? Certainly, when it comes to dissecting the artifice of other movies—of all movies, amazing fabulous, incredibly awful, and everything in between—no other film supplies so many piping-hot slices of meta-commentary goodness just begging to be deployed. Because *Bride* has everything (fencing, fighting, torture, revenge, etcetera, etcetera) and because it knows it has everything, it is the universal movie—all other movies dissolve in it. Look:

Classics: In the 1933 *King Kong,* at the moment when Fay Wray, bound to her sacrificial altar, first sees the giant ape, can't you just hear an imaginary narrator intoning, "Anne's emptiness consumed her. Although the law of the land gave Kong the right to choose his bride, she did not love him"?

Foreign: While watching *Run Lola Run,* don't you wanna cry out, "Wait, wait, you're telling it wrong! She gets the money for Manni, I just know it..."?

Indie: In *Memento,* don't you kinda expect one of Guy Pearce's Polaroid memos to himself to read: "You are not lefthanded"?

Big-budget action: In *Raiders of the Lost Ark,* when Indy and Marion are sealed into the Well of Souls, isn't there a voice assuring us, "They don't get killed by the snakes at this time"?

Crime drama: In *The Silence of the Lambs,* isn't there a moment when Agent Starling is interrogating Lecter in his cell when he says, "Plato, Aristotle, Socrates? Morons"?

Hollywood romantic comedy: In *Jerry Maguire,* shouldn't Renée Zellweger and Tom Cruise have an exchange like this at the end of the film: "I will never doubt again" / "There will never be a need"?

> **Science fiction:** In *2001: A Space Odyssey*, when the astronauts are discussing the supposedly defective AE-35 unit with Hal, don't you think Hal wants to tell them, "You're trying to trick me into giving away something—it won't work..."?

And so on.

An ungenerous fool would say that *The Princess Bride* is full of clichés. I am not an ungenerous fool, so I would clearly never say such a thing. What we call clichés—lucky escapes from death, for instance, or the arrogance of villains—became clichés because the first few times they were used in the cause of telling a ripping yarn, it was discovered that they work really damn well to entertain us. For many films, that's enough—a ticking bomb counting down to the hero's moment of inevitable triumph is good enough, and never mind if the audience has seen that a thousand times before. It may be a cheap cardboard plot, but that satisfies plenty moviegoers most of the time. But every aspect of *Bride*, from William Goldman's script to Rob Reiner's direction to the performances of the cast, is consumed with excising the cardboard from the clichés and finding the core of what continues to be exciting and fascinating about them even after we've seen them a thousand times. And the film does this in a way that could have been disastrous: Instead of trying to hide the fact that it's all stereotype and formula and cliché, the film embraces its formulaic basis with a grand passion, as if it's Goldman et al saying, "We love movies so much, we're even in love the equations that make them run."

Take one scene, as a fer-instance: Goldman's script very carefully sets up, via Westley's explanation for Vizzini, the elusive qualities of iocane powder, the perfect poison—colorless, odorless, tasteless, impossible to detect, and, as we witness, almost instantly fatal. This, truly, is a weapon any of Agatha Christie's—or John Grisham's—killers would, well, kill for. It would confound police and private eyes alike, cause *CSI* laboratory nerds to throw their hands up in frustration, and generally be cause of celebration in the criminal underworld. Free murder!

We also know, though, being experienced consumers of fiction, that no fictional universe can stand for such a perfect weapon—it is but a roadblock in the path of the genius detective who will ultimately unravel the mystery. Sherlock Holmes would refer to an obscure monograph on iocane, probably one he'd written himself. Gil Grissom would devise a lab test to detect the undetectable. It'd take time, but it would be inevitable.

But what happens? "Iocane. I'd bet my life on it." Prince Humperdinck identifies the iocane instantly completely on the basis of its lack of identifiable qualities!

There's an intellectually delicious back-and-forth happening in that one moment: such a deduction is not entirely outrageous, since we have already witnessed some of Humperdinck's extraordinary investigative skills ("Someone has beaten a giant"), but it also instantly cuts the legs out from under one tried-and-true movie trope, the search for clues and the formation of conclusions based on those clues. We expect such things to be based on something we, the audience, can see, clues we're aware of but the detective is not yet privy to, and our enjoyment of the resolution of the mystery comes partly from appreciating the detective's cleverness and partly from being ahead of him, even though he's supposedly much smarter than we are. (If he weren't, he wouldn't be the hero—or villain—of a film!)

But as it would be for Holmes or Grissom, the outcome of Humperdinck's inquiry is foregone, even if he is a bad guy: there is no question that Humperdinck will deduce Westley's game, and because the deduction itself is relatively unimportant to the plot, Goldman can skip all the perfunctory business in the middle and jump right to the end, giving us a witty turnabout regarding the impossibility of Humperdinck's sleuthing talents as well as a joke about what we expect from this kind of situation in a movie.

From how we as the audience react to a movie to how the people in it behave, *Bride* strips away what's clichéd about the clichés, and what's left behind are little gems of snark simply pleading to be put to good use. Whether we've got a problem with a film's pacing (Inigo's "Sir, sir? We're in a terrible rush" to Miracle Max; or "Skip on to the Fire Swamp—that sounded good") or with tricksy flashbacks ("It was ten days till the wedding"), there's a perfect quote. Whether we're appreciating the comeuppance of bad guys ("Humiliations galore!") or the deliciously ridiculous brilliance of detectives ("There was a mighty duel"), there's a quote. There's even a quote that acknowledges the unfeasibility of making a living as a character in a movie ("There's not a lot of money in revenge").

And where did many of these clichés come from in the first place? Two words: fairy tales.

VI

"It was a fine time for me…"

I've heard some less than enthusiastic reactions to *The Princess Bride* that dismiss it as a "kids' movie." Other nonfans see it as mere fluff, a disposable trifle. At best, its less than rabid adherents might concede it is a passably pleasant light comedy. But that is far too small and stifling an assessment of the film—it is, in fact, nothing so simple or so insignificant. *The Princess Bride* holds such a strong grip on the imaginations of so many movie lovers not merely because it is funny and witty and charming and diverting but also because it touches on some of the most elementary aspects of what it means to be alive: the film is basic in the most important and urgent sense. It is about the most primal and powerful and positive of human emotions—love—and also about the basest and most negative: cowardice. It is about the expansive human desire to go exploring and adventuring, and about the defensive human instinct to nest and snuggle in and make a home. It is about the conflicting desires that drive us. It is, under the deadpan humor and abundant cynicism and casual insouciance, primeval.

The film is, as many critics and fans have noted, a deconstruction of fairy tales, one that is so successful at this task that it "out-*Shrek*ed *Shrek*," as Scott Renshaw, film critic and entertainment editor of the alt-newspaper *Salt Lake City Weekly,* says. But in the process of breaking down the clichés of good and evil, love and hate, magic and fate, the film cannot help but itself be about these very same things, nor can it avoid utilizing the very same conventions and formulas that concern the object of the film's satire. Even as we make fun of the essential elements of the folktales that transcend culture and ethnicity to show up all over the world, these elements cannot help but touch us at the same time. These stories, in their most fundamental forms, are so important to our identities as human beings that it may well be impossible to frame a story around them that can truly deflate them, no matter how hard it wants to.

The Princess Bride resonates on such a deep level in part because of the thick, rich veins of mythic ore that run throughout. We recognize the characters and situations—we've met these figures before, in other stories and myths... We know these people. Archetypal projections mean no one needs to explain to us that Buttercup will remain pure at all costs, or that Westley will never waver in integrity or in courage—not a lot of suspense there. We are already predisposed to embrace these characters.
—Stephen Gerringer, Campbellian folklorist and "Practical Campbell" columnist

It's more than merely little things, like how Westley's climbing the rope at the Cliffs of Insanity, following Fezzik the giant, can't help but remind the viewer of Jack climbing his beanstalk to meet his dangerously large adversary. The warp and weft of the movie is inescapably folklorish. The Grandfather's line about the book he's reading to his Grandson containing all the important bits a good story needs—"fencing, fighting, torture, revenge, giants, monsters, chases, escapes, true love, miracles!"—is just as true when it comes to the elements of the basic fairy tale: they're all here. Secret identities, magicians, an evil prince, a kindly king, a castle, the woods, a princess, a pirate, a giant, a swordsman, rival suitors, feats of strength and feats of intelligence. (The Grandfather's reading, in fact, evokes the oral tradition of fairy tales, which were most likely first created in their original renditions and passed around long before writing was ever even conceived of.) Buttercup is sister to Cinderella, a lowly commoner who catches the eye of royalty, and Snow White, charming and lovely but not very bright. She is, as girls and women tend to be in these first of all stories, little more than a trophy for a man, or, in this case, two men. Humperdinck is the more untraditional example of this stereotype: his motives are not pure and he does not love Buttercup, seeing only her political value as a prize. Her relationship with Westley, though, is downright clichéd in its essentials: as the story opens, she is intended as his reward for finding his fortune; later, she is his reward for his bravery in rescuing her. That true love truly binds them does not change this dynamic—she is not a fully developed character; she is, she readily admits herself, "a silly girl."

The film may be called *The Princess Bride*, but in fact it is in many ways Westley's tale, and an excellent—if somewhat truncated—example of the mythological hero and his journey from innocence through adversity and onto sophistication, as described by comparative mythologist and folklorist Joseph Campbell in his book *The Hero with a Thousand Faces.* If some of *Bride*'s power springs from the sense that, for all its goofy outrageousness, there is something very elemental in it, this is why: the archetype of the hero and the model of his journey forms the core of many stories that transcend time and culture. If there's something naggingly familiar about this story, in some remote and fundamental way that breathes authority into it and leaves it lingering in the imagination, it's because similar elements resonate through many powerful stories that we are intimate with, from that of Jesus to that of Luke Skywalker. Silly stuff aside, there's something that just feels right about *Bride,* and this is why: it is classic in a way that goes far beyond its borrowings of fairy-tale clichés.

In another major joke of Goldman's, though, most of the very

It has become a movie that parents watch with their children. And over the years, as the children grow up, they start to appreciate the sophistication of the humor and the satire, and they become adults who then show it to their children. Any number of people that I run into that are now of postcollege age—23, 24, 25—say they watch it with their nieces and nephews, and they still have a wonderful, warm, fond place in their heart for the movie. So, there's a crossgenerational appeal, because we adults love fairy tales, too. We realize that it's a story that has fun with itself, without making fun of itself—or, rather, with the genre.
—**actor Chris Sarandon, aka "Prince Humperdinck," in an interview with the author**

important middle section of the story is simply not presented to us. We first meet Westley as the laconic Farm Boy, poor but perfect in Buttercup's eyes but presumably recognizing in himself something of a naivete in the ways of the world, since he feels the need to go off into the dangerous unknown—where bitter challenges and certain death are sure to lurk—and find out what he is made of as a man before he can be worthy of betrothing himself to a woman. But when we next meet Westley, his journey is complete—he has returned to his old world transformed. Westley is now, literally, a man of the world: a learned commander of his inferiors, a legend with a fearsome reputation (if one he only partially earned himself), a wit, even. How he was transformed is something of which we are allowed only tantalizing hints and glimpses. It's tantamount to telling the story of Jesus by jumping from his carefree work as a carpenter to his arrest by Roman soldiers. It's as if we never saw Luke Skywalker again after he left Tatooine until he confronts the Emperor on the rebuilt Death Star.

In most stories that take the hero's journey as their template, the bulk of the tale is taken up with the trials and tribulations that turn him from a callow youth into a mature man. But as with the many other ancient conventions of storytelling, Goldman thumbs his nose at this one, too: If Westley's successful completion of this ritual of old is not in question (as Buttercup's survival of the eels is also not), then there's no need to muck around in all that tedious story and—as the Grandson implores his Grandfather—skip on to the good bits. And the good bits are the last hurdles Westley must surmount, a few final challenges that are not required to prove his manhood—he has, in the mythological calculus that underpins these stories, already done that, and indeed, he has so matured that the woman who loves him does not recognize him merely because he wears a mask. (One imagines those "eyes like the sea after a storm" would be fairly memorable; or perhaps Buttercup is even dumber than she seems. In his DVD commentary, director Reiner likens Buttercup's nonrecognition of Westley to the precedent established by Superman, for whom a pair of glasses suffices as a disguise... But nah: it's funnier if Buttercup is just dumb as a post.)

Instead, Westley's ordeals in the film are meant to sweep away the very means by which he accomplished this feat of maturation: the persona of the Dread Pirate Roberts. It's wickedly funny, the concept of a name and reputation being passed from one man to another ("No one would surrender to the Dread Pirate Westley"), but it's also profoundly insightful: it is very much symbolic of the ways in which human wisdom is handed down from generation to generation, a combination of the empowerment and permission the elder gives the younger to go out and explore the world with the necessary freedom for the youngster to do so on his own, to chart his own course from that point on and to succeed or fail through his own capability or lack thereof. It's telling that Westley hands off the Dread Pirate Roberts persona to Inigo, for while

---

I am in awe of how skillfully the film reimagines this ancient motif in a way that seems fresh yet familiar, bringing it out of storyland and into the real world. What elements of the hero's journey appear in movie aren't consciously contrived to fit a prescribed formula, but seem rather to reflect the spontaneous, natural outpouring of Goldman's imagination as he played with this genre.
—Stephen Gerringer

Inigo is physically a grown man, he has never really matured beyond the eleven-year-old who dedicated his life to avenging his father's unjust death. With that task accomplished, Inigo is ready to strike out on his own hero's journey, to truly and at last take the path to independent adulthood.

So, Westley has only some minor trials to endure—treacherous enough on their own, but far smaller in scale than what he went through as the valet of Ryan (aka the Dread Pirate Roberts III) and hardly constituting an ongoing test of his manhood in the way that, perhaps, being threatened with death every evening at bedtime is ("I'll most likely kill you in the morning"). And those tasks number a very traditional three, a figure that recurs frequently in mythology, from the tales collected by the Brothers Grimm to modern stories with mythic import, such as the three contests of the Triwizard Tournament in *Harry Potter and the Goblet of Fire.* Westley, of course, must defeat Inigo with his sword, Fezzik with his strength, and Vizzini with his brain... and if those opponents who do not die at his hand later become his allies, well, that's traditional, too. Likewise, the three terrors of the Fire Swamp—there's that number again—are mere bumps in the road, small obstacles keeping him and Buttercup apart until he can clear away the remnants of the even greater challenges he has already faced, the ones we have not been witness to. This incarnation of the Dread Pirate Roberts must die before Westley can take up his new life.

And die he does, in what is perhaps the most essential torment the hero on his journey must suffer: death and resurrection. Maybe Count Rugen's Machine renders Westley "only mostly dead," a state from which of course any old body might return. But a miracle might not be needed for the ordinary man who was still a little alive. And when Westley has been resurrected—thanks to the doings of Miracle Max, who rightly predicted that it would take a miracle—he is already shrugging off his disguise: Fezzik plays the Dread Pirate Roberts in their subsequent assault on the castle to rescue Buttercup. Westley, to whom no one would surrender, has returned, but he is no longer a mere farmboy: he is now a force to be reckoned with.

VII

"Murdered by pirates is good..."

A reader of my film-review Web site FlickFilosopher.com once emailed me to ask: How can Westley be a hero if he murders people?

To which the only proper response surely is: "Well, duh..."

VII (CON'T)
MURDERED BY PIRATES: STILL GOOD

I did not, in fact, say "Well, duh" to my curious correspondent. Let me 'splain.

No, is too much. Let me sum up.

Readers of my film criticism at FlickFilosopher.com know in what high regard I hold *The Princess Bride*: it is No. 3 on the publicly posted list of my own personal all-time top 100 movies. And of course I cannot help but drop lines from the film into my reviews sometimes, for—as I've previously noted—there is hardly an occasion, particularly when one is talking about movies, for which a quote from *The Princess Bride* is not appropriate.

Similarly, however, my disdain for the science fiction action film *Pitch Black* is also widely known, and not something that I'm at all embarrassed about even though in some circles *Pitch Black* is looked upon with a reverence that, if it is not the equal of the esteem in which *Bride* is held, is at least a far more intense reaction than most movies typically prompt.

Let me quote from my own review of *Pitch Black*:

> [T]he truly offensive thing about Pitch Black *is the fact that Riddick—remember, the psycho killer?—is the hero here. This is a man who obviously enjoys threatening everyone around him. He is not someone who committed a murder, say, in self-defense or even inadvertently in commission of another crime, like a robbery, and that's why he was in custody. This is a man who gets off on the fear he instills in the rest of the movie's characters. And his menacing is played for laughs. He taunts Johns, thrusting a gun in the other man's face, and cracks a catchphrase-style joke. When the teenage passenger starts to emulate Riddick, shaving his head like Riddick's and sporting the same sunglasses, this is meant to be an appropriate, and humorous, homage to a killer. And lest we be tempted to try to find something to soften Riddick as a character, to try to make him more palatable,* Pitch Black's *posters and advertising remind us to "Fight Evil with Evil." And this is the character we're supposed to cheer on.*

My reader wanted to know how I could justify my adoration of Westley—whom, we are told, takes no prisoners and leaves no survivors—in light of my contempt for the murderous Riddick's status as a "hero."

The simplest answer is this: The only person we actually witness Westley killing is Vizzini, and one could argue that this was a life-or-death situation. The Sicilian was in the midst of committing a violent felony—kidnapping—and had to be stopped by any means necessary. This seems hardly to be the kind of killing that should prevent anyone from assuming the mantle of "hero"—and in fact, it's usually precisely the kind of killing that conveys hero status. What's more, we also witness Westley not killing when he could have, and perhaps been justified in doing so: he leaves Inigo and Fezzik alive after their trials by combat, when the medieval code of justice under which the land of Florin presumably functions may perhaps have granted him a perfectly moral right (in the understanding of the time) to slay his defeated opponents. But he does not do so. He also does not kill Humperdinck, when he has perhaps even greater moral justification to do so.

In fact, the only evidence we have that Westley is an indiscriminate murderer of innocents are his own words and the reputation that precedes him. But, assuming for the moment that he does not leave a trail of bodies in his wake, it would be contrary to his own best interests to correct such a misapprehension. Because, as we know, once word gets round that a pirate's gone soft, it's nothing but work, work, work all the time. Perhaps the very first Dread Pirate Roberts really did kill everyone he met, hence earning the fearsome reputation his successors have assumed—it's easy to see how no further killing would be required: it would make more sense to turn tail and run at the first sign of Roberts and leave him to whatever treasure he wishes. Though perhaps even that first Dread Pirate Roberts was more choosy when it came to his victims: it's also contrary to a pirate's best interests to slay everyone he meets, for who, then, would be left to spread the dire tale of a pirate who takes no prisoners? As was pointed out in the *Princess Bride*–esque film *Pirates of the Caribbean: Curse of the Black Pearl*, someone's got to survive if such an awful reputation is to spread. The concept of a famous criminal who takes no prisoners and leaves no witnesses is untenable.

But so are Machines that suck your life away, Rodents Of Unusual Size, chocolate-coated miracle pills, and anyone in a pseudomedieval pseudo Europe knowing that Australia is populated by convicts, which would not happen until the late 18th century. The slightly more metaphysical answer to the apparent dilemma of Westley's heroism is not merely that his story is fiction but that it is a fiction within a fiction—there is an extra layer of unreality to shield it from the rules we live by in the real world. *Pitch Black*, on the other hand, wants its audience to forget is "only" a story and intends for it to be taken as literal, for all that it takes place on an alien planet and involves fighting creatures that are entirely fantastical. *Bride* is very self-consciously aware that it is all a sham. It is deliberately absurd.

And that's the real answer: *The Princess Bride* is absurd. You can't watch a play by Beckett or Ionesco or Pinter without catching on to its perception-altering weirdness, even if you don't understand the point of the weirdness—but you can watch and enjoy and memorize and worship *The Princess Bride* perfectly well without ever realizing that it is very much an example of the bewildered existentialism that gripped those playwrights in the wake of the devastation of World War II. *Bride* is, of course, a cartoon version of Theater of the Absurd—call it Movie of the Absurd—larger and broader and far more colorful and nowhere near as overtly challenging as the plotless, illogical plays full of gibberish dialogue with which Beckett and Ionesco and Pinter provoked audiences. *Bride* is a primer, an elementary lesson book on absurd philosophy, but it wraps it in an almost familiar, almost childlike, very charming fairy tale—so it's easy not to see how absurd-with-a-capital-A it truly is.

"One of the most important aspects of absurd drama was its distrust of language as a means of communication." So says Dr. Jan Culík—lecturer in Czech literature, culture, politics, and media at the University of Glasgow's School of Modern Languages and Cultures—in his enlightening essay "The Theatre of the Absurd: The West and the East" [www2.arts.gla.ac.uk/Slavonic/Absurd. htm]. How much we can trust what Westley says about himself, particularly in the light of lack of evidence to support what he says, is therefore a matter of debate.

But our ability—or inability—to trust him is less indicative of the absurdity of *Bride* than is the film's turning death and suffering into a running joke. Theater of the Absurd is obsessed with the torment and despair that arises from what it sees as an inexplicability of the universe and a meaninglessness of human life: there is no better summation of such an attitude than when Westley's sneers to Buttercup, "Life is pain, Highness. Anyone who says differently is selling something." The randomness of pain and suffering could not better be encapsulated than by Westley's explanation of how he was treated by his mentor Dread Pirate Roberts: "Good night, Westley. Good work. Sleep well. I'll most likely kill you in the morning." For that to be followed almost immediately by Westley's cheerful "It was a fine time for me..." is ridiculous and absurd and gets a laugh for the stark contrast it presents, the constant threat of violent death constituting a "fine time." It is Absurd because it is characterized by a sense of the incomprehensibility of life—who knows what to expect from anything?—and of the unfathomableness of people, who aren't what they seem ("'I am not the Dread Pirate Roberts,' he said.") and don't even tell the truth half the time.

Westley is an Absurd hero not only because he is philosophical about pain or because we like and admire him even though he embodies all the trust we cannot place in others, who lie about their motives and actions and even about their names. Westley is an Absurd hero because he triumphs over those who represent the precise opposite of the Absurd notions that the universe is unknowable and life is pointless. His victory is the victory of emotion over reason, of anarchy over order, of the heart over the mind. Westley upsets the rationalistic egotism of the idea that the universe is knowable—the elevation of Westley to hero is an embracing of joyful chaos.

Vizzini's downfall, for instance, is his arrogance, his unshakable belief that he knows everything about everything and hence is untrickable. Vizzini sees reason and order in the universe, and believes he can use logic to see him through any eventuality, including being confronted by a very assured poisoner who is unfazed even by Vizzini's "obvious" genius. Vizzini's torturous argument with himself as he tries to tease out in which wine goblet Westley has placed the poison is hilarious on its face: any viewer can clearly appreciate that his one-man debate does not even remotely cover all the possibilities inherent in the situation. ("Criminals are used to having people not trust them, as you are not trusted by me, so I can clearly not choose the wine in front of you.") And so Vizzini's confidence in himself grows increasingly misplaced. Except that he cannot see that. His clockwork world allows for nothing unexpected. There is no "logic" in a man poisoning his own drink, so that contingency never occurs to Vizzini. And that's what kills him: his reliance on an outmoded understanding of the universe. Vizzini's universe is all gears and cogs, very 18th century; Westley's is about quantum uncertainty, ahead of its time in 1987 to be very 21st century.

(Consider this: Perhaps Westley does not kill Inigo at the conclusion of their duel because he sees in the Spaniard a soul in simpatico with his own. If Inigo is not lefthanded but is aware enough of the absurdity of the universe to try to trick an opponent with such a ruse, then he is a man in touch with the impenetrable nature of the universe, and hence worthy of life.)

Prince Humperdinck, too, relishes the feeling that everything is under his control. "I've got my country's 500th anniversary to plan, my wedding to arrange, my wife to murder, and Guilder to frame for it—I'm swamped." There is no room for chance events in his mind, and even in the face of the reality of the chaotic and random nature of the universe, as his plans fall prey to unplanned-for circumstance and the unwillingness of other players to cooperate, he sees all as working to his benefit: "When I hired Vizzini to have her murdered on our engagement day, I thought that was clever. But it's going to be so much more moving when I strangle her on our wedding night." As with Vizzini's arrogance, Humperdinck's will eventually lead to his doom—not death, but humiliation, of course, but also a peculiar comeuppance that points out how futile it is to deal with the world rationally: he finds himself surrendering to a man to which no one else would ever, ever surrender.

(Something else to consider: The dual nature of Westley's

character is very much in keeping with the indeterministic understanding of the universe he represents. Is he the farmboy Westley, to whom no one would ever surrender because he a nobody without a reputation? Or is he the Dread Pirate Roberts, to whom no one would ever surrender because it would mean certain death? Of course, he's both at the same time—like Schödinger's cat, alive and dead at the same time until an observer causes the field of probability to collapse into an actuality, Westley's disposition is unknown until we truly observe him, which happens over the course of the film, until his field of probability collapses into his new actuality: he is neither farmboy nor pirate but a new man entirely.)

All the humor that arises out of the contradictions of the characters and the ironies in what they say is very much an aspect of absurdity. Culík points out that absurd drama "assumed a highly unusual, innovative form" and was part of an allegorical, mythic "tradition of the world as a stage and life as a dream," one that "sought to express the individual's longing for a single myth of general validity." Perhaps we might even consider it a "dweam within a dweam" as *Bride* is a fiction within a fiction. The toying with levels of reality—and with levels of self-conscious falsity—and the undercutting of the conventions of storytelling that *Bride* engages in clearly mark it as powerfully influenced by absurd thinking. (The innovative use of cliché I yakked about in Chapter V? Culík says: "Absurd drama uses conventionalised speech, clichés, slogans and technical jargon, which is distorts, parodies and breaks down.") Can we trust anything we see on the screen in *Bride*? After all, we see that the Grandfather is reading from a book, but we never see the pages of that book. How do we know that what he's purporting to read are the words that are actually on the pages of that book? Especially when we know that he's willing to skip over some parts and truncate others? It's entirely possible, with the shaky foundation the film rests on, that nothing in the medieval story is "true" or "real" or an even semiaccurate representation of "S. Morgenstern's *The Princess Bride*." It could all be eight levels of nonsense.

In fact, nonsense writers such as Edward Lear and Lewis Carroll were forerunners of modern Absurdists... and as Culík notes, "one of the greatest masters of nonsense poetry was," ahem, "the German poet Christian Morgernstern." Coincidence? Absurdists would say yes: if everything is random and meaningless, then coincidences can have no significance. But screenwriter William Goldman isn't a die-hard absurdist—he is, to coin a term, postabsurd. Absurdity is about hopelessness and despair in the face of the pointlessness of existence—there is no joyfulness in the chaos for the Absurdists. Goldman, though, has hope and does not despair: "Life isn't fair," Goldman notes at the end of his novel *The Princess Bride*; "it's just fairer than death, that's all." It's possible that Goldman may see the universe itself as pointless and wracked with pain, but he also sees a point for us insignificant creatures who reside in it.

It's like this: Westley's threat to leave Humperdinck, the putative villain, "wallowing in freakish misery forever" naturally bothers Humperdinck more than the idea of a quick death—in an absurd universe, that's exactly how it should be. If life is pain and meaninglessness, why bother with living? Why not just have it done and over with? A life of pain is a far greater punishment than death and the blissful oblivion that follows.

But the threat of a lifetime of pain is certainly absurd too: if life is pain, then we are all doomed to a lifetime of pain, so how would a post "to the pain" Humperdinck really be in any more torment than the rest of us? The difference here is that the lifetime of pain Westley promises Humperdinck specifically includes not just physical torment but social ostracism. Humperdinck would be excluded from the one reason to hope and to take joy in this hopeless, absurd universe: love. (Goldman again, from the book: "I really do think that love is the best thing in the world, except for cough drops.")

The real villain of *Bride* may well be Count Rugen, who is more like Westley, in some ways, than any other character: he is Westley's mirror image, as a truly villainous counterpart for a truly heroic hero should be, far more so than Humperdinck or Vizzini. Like Westley, he has clearly given a great deal of thought to the subject of pain—he has a "deep and abiding interest" in it and is in fact "writing the definitive work on the subject." Rugen recognizes the pain of life and embraces it, as if he sees no other option in an absurd universe. Westley, on the other hand, recognizes the pain—because who can truly avoid or deny it?—but he throws true love in its face.

True love is what makes the pain of life endurable, perhaps even conquerable. "Ultimate suffering" is not death or physical pain but the loss of true love, as Inigo notes: the Man in Black's "true love is marrying another tonight, so who else has the cause for ultimate suffering?" (How Inigo knows Buttercup is the Man

> Fairy tales are very important because they're myths that contain little morality tales—there's a reason that they've remained popular for so long.
> **—actor Cary Elwes, aka "Westley," in "As You Wish"**

in Black's true love is a mystery, though I confess this did not occur to me until very recently; my previous dozens of viewings of the film had somehow hidden this little plot hole from my eyes.) Humperdinck does not fear death because he does not have true love in his life, but when Miracle Max asks Westley, our absurd hero—or, perhaps, postabsurd hero—what he's got to live for, his answer is "true love."

But all of this is just so much intellectual masturbation. No one watches *The Princess Bride* a hundred times because it tickles them to see the connection to Pinter. The viewer doesn't need to know anything at all about existentialistic philosophy or modern avant garde drama, need never have even heard the term "Theater of the Absurd" to understand, if only on a subconscious level, the profundity of a line like "It was a fine time for me" or the wrongness of Vizzini's reasoning. We all live amidst the violence and disorder of modern life—we all live in the same supremely messed-up world that prompted the absurdists to write their plays about the senselessness of life and the chaos of the universe. But the reason truly absurd drama will never catch on as a popular entertainment is that most people don't agree with its conclusions: life isn't pointless, at least not on a personal level, and there indeed are things to live for. Those things may be illusions and fantasies, but they're comforting illusions and fantasies that make the pain of life endurable.

And that's the genius of Goldman's postabsurdity. It says, Yes, life is pain and the world is a disaster and danger lurks around every corner, but love is good. That's a sentiment that almost no one would disagree with. Though you might have a tough time getting some of us to admit that...

VIII

"THIS IS TRUE LOVE—YOU THINK
THIS HAPPENS EVERY DAY?"

I had an interesting little exchange with Mandy Patinkin—
Okay, can I just interrupt here and go, Woo-hoo? Yes, I spoke to Mandy Patinkin in the course of writing this book. He was kind enough to give of his time (as was Chris Sarandon) and was very helpful in focusing some of my thoughts on *The Princess Bride* (as was Chris), but did I melt into a puddle of fangirl goo when he said to me—to me!—in the course of chatting about the film, "Hello, my name is Inigo Montoya..."? Of course I did. He related a charming tale about meeting a particular kind of fan today, twenty years after shooting the movie:

> *I think my favorite thing is when little kids come up to*

me, and their parents say, "You know who this is?" And
they look like, "No. There's this salt-and-peppered, with-
a-bald-spot guy... Who is this guy?" And then I lean over
to the kid, and I whisper in their ear, "Hello! My name is
Inigo Montoya." And they just don't know what's going
on! It's so much fun.

And if you can imagine the look on a little kid's face at that
moment... well, then you can imagine the look on mine, too. And
I knew full well who Mandy was.

So, now that I've gotten the name-dropping out of the way...

I had an interesting little exchange with Mandy Patinkin, and
it went like this:

MAJ: I'm hoping to be telling the truth about the movie.
MP: Okay! It's a fairy tale, though, so you're not under
    any obligation...

But I did feel an obligation, even if it was only a self-imposed
one: I set out to find the truth about *The Princess Bride.* Not the
facts—I wasn't interested in silly things that happened on the set
or the goofy things that fans do to demonstrate their devotion. I
wanted to unwrap the power of the film itself, figure out what it is
about this movie that has enthralled so many people for so long.
Why are so many people so in love with this film?

I didn't know the answer when I started. Oh, I had little parts
of the answer—the movie is funny, it's swashbuckling, it's full of
mystery and magic, it's romantic. But that could be said about
lots of movies, even if few manage to combine so many disparate

elements so well. Okay, yes, the film is about that very special thing, true love, which, as Westley points out, doesn't happen every day. My new buddy Mandy told me:

> *Every single frame, every single word, every single individual's journey in the film is about their desire to conquer true love. Whether it be for a child's version of the fantasy, or the more double entendre meanings for the grownups, I think it's the quest for true love [that inspires the audience's devotion for the film]...*

Campbellian folklorist Stephen Gerringer agrees:

> *On one level,* The Princess Bride *is an entertaining tale of adventure, intrigue, and romance. But on another level, a wisdom level, it does not speak exclusively of romantic love, but of something more, that which fuels romantic love: true love. Whether of handsome youth for maiden fair, or grandpa for grandson—as we see when Fred Savage suggests Peter Falk might return to read the story again tomorrow...*

But... but... no one would deny that *The Princess Bride* is about all kinds of true love, right? (More examples: the familial love of Inigo for his father, the loving friendship of Fezzik and Inigo). I mean, that's no secret, is it? Anyone who's seen the film, even those who don't get it, could have figured that out. How can that be the answer? And what if it is about true love? Lots of movies are about love, even, purportedly, true love—how many movies don't end in swooning clinches between the hero and heroine that are meant to imply that at last this meant-to-be-together couple can ride off into the sunset to live and love in bliss forever? What's the difference between those movies and *The Princess Bride*?

Here's the secret: *We don't believe those other movies* when they talk about love, not really. No matter how honest and how sincere and how impassioned they are, those movies are fake, and we know it. Their honesty and sincerity ends up working against them, in a way, particularly for us. Remember when I said we *Bride* fans were cynics? Our cynicism prevents us from buying that lovey-dovey stuff. Oh, maybe for the course of a movie (a lesser movie than *Bride,* that is), we'll grudgingly allow ourselves to be swept away, but as soon as the movie is over, our doubt and scorn kick in: "That's all fine and good for fictional characters, I suppose," we tell ourselves, "all the kissing nonsense, but here in the real world, it never works out." Not that we don't want it to—it just never does, not in the hopelessly idealistic and dreamy way movies usually act like it must invariably do. All those other people, the ones who think that metaphoric knights in shining armor really do ride to the rescue of figurative damsels in distress before they both ride

---

[*The Princess Bride* evinces a] cynicism that paves the way for something heartfelt. It disarms the viewer with its sarcasm—you know it's not putting you on. It takes a lot of skill to use cynicism and sarcasm to weed away cheap idealisms in order to encourage deeper ones...
**—film critic Jeffrey Chen,
LVJeffrey's Window to the Movies
[windowtothemovies.com]**

---

off into a symbolic gorgeous sunset? All those other people, who really do believe in real-life fairy tales? They can keep their fantasy romances and their sappy happy endings, and if that's what makes them happy, bully for them.

But we ain't buying it. We know, as Humperdinck does, that not one couple in a century has the chance for genuine happiness, no matter what the storybooks say. Come at us with saccharine sweetness, and we don't believe it—the real world isn't like that. But come at us with an attitude that reflects how we really feel about the cold, hard, cruel world? Sarcasm, we get. Pessimism, we get. "Life is pain"? Oh boy, do we get that. But if even amidst all that pain and ultimate suffering true love can thrive, then, wow, maybe happiness can exist after all.

It's no coincidence that the few other love stories that cynics will admit to finding genuinely romantic are ones that don't sugarcoat the pain of life or pretend that even the truest of true love can survive it. *Casablanca's* Rick Blaine, for instance, is one of cinema's legendary curmudgeons, for whom life is pain and true love is the only thing that melts his ice-hard heart (if only briefly). *Titanic's* framing story gives us Rose Dawson's grand romance only as she tells it to a skeptical audience of deep-ocean salvagers—as they are slowly won over, so are we. (Oh, and Rose's true love? He dies in the end, and he stays all dead... though death does not stop their true love—it only delays it for a while.)

The Princess Bride? This one leaves them all behind. It's the ultimate love story for die-hard cynics who don't believe in love stories. It's selling the idea of true love, sure, but it knows it better than to tell us other but that life is pain in the process.

CASABLANCA, OR THE PRINCESS REFUGEE

SUP. MAP OF NAZI-OCCUPIED EUROPE

NEWSREEL NARRATOR
Let me 'splain. No, there is too
much. Let me sum up. The Germans
are descending on free Casablanca
in little less than half an hour.
So all our Nazi-fighting heroes
have to do is sneak in, find out
who has the stolen documents,
buy the letters of transit, make
their escape... after they break
Rick Blaine's heart.

EXT. AIRPORT RUNWAY

RENAULT, THE
FRENCH POLICE
CHIEF
(showing off for
the arriving Nazi
officers)
I want the Thieves' Oasis
emptied!

INT. RICK'S CAFE AMERICAIN

REFUGEE
(attempting to sell
smuggled diamonds)
I hate to wait. I don't suppose
you could speed things up?

BLACK MARKETEER
(taking his time
examining the
jewels)
I could do that. But I do not
think you would accept my offer,
since I am only waiting around to
cheat you.

REFUGEE
That does put a damper on our
relationship.

LATER

RICK
All right, where are the letters
of transit? The battle of wits
has begun.

RENAULT
But it's so simple. All I have to
do is divine from what I know of
you: are you the sort of man who
would hide contraband in his own
drinking establishment? Now, a
clever man would hide the goods
at his own business, because he
would know that only a great fool
would bother to search so obvious
a place. I am not a great fool,
so I should clearly not order an
official ransacking of your bar.
But you must have known I was not
a great fool, you would have
(con't)

counted on it, so I can clearly
assume that the documents are
actually hidden here at Rick's.

EVEN LATER

                STRASSER, THE
                NAZI OFFICER
Who are you?

                RICK
No one of consequence.

                STRASSER
I must know...

                RICK
Get used to disappointment.

                STRASSER
Okay.

FLASHBACK: PARIS

                NARRATOR
Aduwtewy, that dweam wifin a
dweam...

                AUDIENCE
Boo! Boo! Boo!

                ILSA
Why do you do this?

                    AUDIENCE
Because you had love in your
hands, and you gave it up.

                    ILSA
But they would have killed Rick
if I hadn't done it.

                    AUDIENCE
Your true love lives. Even if
you're married to another.
          (to one another)
True love saved her in Paris, and
she treated it like garbage. And
that's what she is, the Queen
of Refuse. So bow down to her
if you want, bow to her. Bow to
the Queen of Slime, the Queen of
Filth, the Queen of Putrescence!
Boo! Boo! Rubbish! Filth! Slime!
Muck! Boo! Boo! Boo!

LATER STILL

                    RICK
You fool! You fell victim to one
of the classic blunders! The most
famous is, "Never get involved in
an underground resistance in war-
torn Europe," but only slightly
less well-known is this: "Never
go in against a Nazi when death
is on the line!" You think your
dearest love will save you?

> ILSA
>
> I never said he was my dearest
> love. And yes, he will save me.
> That I know.

> RICK
>
> You admit to me you do not love
> your husband?

> ILSA
>
> He knows I do not love him.

> RICK
>
> Are not capable of love is what
> you mean.

> ILSA
>
> I have loved more deeply than a
> cynic like yourself could ever
> dream.

FERRARI'S OFFICE

> VICTOR
>
> Are you the criminal mastermind
> who ruled Casablanca all those
> years?

> FERRARI
>
> The stinking Nazis took over. And
> thank you so much for bringing
> up such a painful subject. While
> you're at it, why don't you give
> me a nice paper cut and pour
> lemon juice on it? We're closed!

                    VICTOR
We need a miracle. It's very
important.

                    FERRARI
You got money?

                    VICTOR
Sixty-five.

                    FERRARI
Sheesh! I never worked for so
little, except once, and that was
a very noble cause.

                    VICTOR
This is noble, sir. My wife is
crippled. My children are on the
brink of starvation.

                    FERRARI
Are you a rotten liar.

                    VICTOR
I need to avenge my country,
invaded these three years.

                    FERRARI
Your first story was better.
Unless I'm wrong, and I am never
wrong, the letters of transit
are hidden at Rick's. Have fun
storming the cafe!

                    VICTOR
               (to Ilsa)
          You think it'll work?

                    ILSA
          It would take a miracle.

INT. RICK'S APARTMENT - NIGHT

                    ILSA
          If you'll give me the
          documents... whatever you ask
          for payment ... you'll get it, I
          promise you...

                    RICK
          And what is that worth, the
          promise of a woman? You're very
          funny, Ilsa. Now, tell me truly.
          When you found out Victor was
          alive, did you run to him that
          same hour, or did you wait a
          whole week out of respect for the
          brokenhearted?

                    ILSA
          You mocked me once, never do it
          again. I died that day!

                    RICK
          As you wish.

INT. RENAULT'S OFFICE - MORNING

                    VICTOR
          So it's to be torture.

Renault nods.

                    VICTOR
        I can cope with torture.

Renault shakes his head.

                    VICTOR
        You don't believe me?

                    RENAULT
        You survived Nazi Europe. You
        must be very brave. But nobody
        withstands the appeasers.

                    ILSA
        We'll never succeed. We may as
        well die here.

                    VICTOR
        No, no. We have already
        succeeded. I mean, what are the
        three terrors of Casablanca?
        The black marketers—no problem.
        There's a money-grubbing
        chortling surrounding each; we
        can avoid that. Two, Vichy water,
        which you were clever enough to
        discover what that tastes like,
        so in the future we can avoid
        that too.

                    ILSA
        Victor, what about the
        R.O.U.S.es?

                    VICTOR
          Ricks Of Unusual Sentiment? I
          don't think they exist.

Rick enters.

                    RICK
          Will you promise to hurt him?

                    RENAULT
          What was that?

                    VICTOR
          What was that?

                    RICK
          If I admit I have the letters of
          transit and use them to escape
          with Ilsa, will you promise to
          hurt him?

                    RENAULT
          May I live a thousand years and
          never appease again.

EXT. AIRPORT - NIGHT AND FOG

                    RICK
               (to Victor)
          Love her as I have loved her, and
          there will be joy.

                    ILSA
          I will never love again.

AUDIENCE
You filmed that wrong. She doesn't
leave with Victor, she leaves
with Rick. We're just sure of
it. After all that Rick meant to
her, if she doesn't marry him, it
wouldn't be fair.

DIRECTOR
Well, who says life is fair?
Where is that written? Life isn't
always fair.

AUDIENCE
We're telling you, you're messing
up the story. Now get it right!

The plane takes off, leaving Rick and
Renault on the tarmac.

RICK
(above the roar of
the plane taking
off)
That is the sound of ultimate
suffering.

RENAULT
Life is pain, Rick. Anyone who
says differently is selling
something.

DIRECTOR
Isn't that a wonderful ending?

```
            AUDIENCE
        (sarcastic)
    Yeah, it's really good.
        (beat)
    Maybe we could watch it again
    tomorrow?
```

inspired by "Is This a Kissing Book?"—the story of 'The Lord of
the Rings' told only though quotes from 'The Princess Bride'
[mollyringwraith.livejournal.com/44608.html]

IX

"WHEN I WAS YOUR AGE, TELEVISION WAS CALLED BOOKS."

It sounds exhausting to be so cynical when it's laid out bare like that. But of course it isn't, any more so than it is for people who are relentlessly optimistic and happy to be so damn chipper all the time. It's just the way we all are.

There are days, though, or weeks, even, when we see our cynicism justified everywhere we turn. When real-life egotistical Vizzinis and priggish Humperdincks have been thwarting us constantly or we've been mired in a metaphorical Fire Swamp (where office meetings are like lightning sand and the R.O.U.S.es wear three-piece suits) or the seemingly insurmountable Cliffs of Insanity loom before our every endeavor. Those are the times when it becomes an absolutely necessity, a revitalizing act, to come home, sprawl on the sofa, and watch *The Princess Bride* for the 1,309th time. To forget that Buttercup won't get eaten by the eels, that Westley isn't lefthanded either, that the albino's wheelbarrow was left over the albino. To be reminded that storming the castle is fun, that there's not a lot of money in revenge, that Westley is no one to be trifled with. To settle in with absurd people we love— and love to hate—and travel with them through dangerous and beautiful lands and say every line of dialogue along with them.

Movies can be comfort food, no doubt about it, retreats from messy, confusing, disappointing reality to times and places that are simply more fun to be in. Where no matter how many expectations are thwarted before you even know to anticipate them, no matter how many clichés are undermined before you're even aware they've come into play, no matter how much intellectual mucking about with the concepts of storytelling and moviemaking goes on... no matter how much we cynics need a movie that doesn't condescend to unrealistic fantasies about "true love," really true true love actually and finally does win in the end anyway. It's almost as if the film permits us, if not an actual journey into sentimentality, then at least a peek at the diversion other, far more sentimental

> I can't get over that I'm connected to it. I'll never forget: Rob [Reiner] called us and said there was going to be a rough-cut screening, and the minute it was over, I was weeping, and my wife, who was sitting next to me, said, "What's wrong?" I said to her, "I never in my life dreamed that I would ever get to be in something like this."
> **—actor Mandy Patinkin,**
> **aka "Inigo," in an interview with the author**

fantasies bring the less cynical.

So *The Princess Bride* is also a meditation and a mantra for us cynics, a reminder that it's okay to be gloomy and downbeat because, sure, the world definitely deserves to be approached from such an angle... as long as we don't let ourselves give up on the hope of and the search for the one thing, no matter how rare, that makes this painful life worth enduring.

Yes, it's that pesky true-love thing again. But don't rescind my Cynics Club membership card just yet. I will never tire of watching *The Princess Bride,* because I still know there will always be reasons to be cynical. But I also know that there will always be a need to escape them, too.

TWO MEN IN BLACK WALK INTO A BAR...

BARTENDER: You're the Dread Pirate Roberts—admit it.

WESTLEY: With pride. A round for my fellow man-in-black here.

JOHNNY CASH: Hello, I'm Johnny Cash.

WESTLEY [*whispers*]: I am not the Dread Pirate Roberts, but no one would surrender to the Dread Pirate Westley.

[*the bartender brings two shotglasses and a bottle*]

JOHNNY CASH [*toasting*]: I shot a man in Reno just to watch him die.

WESTLEY: Do you always begin conversations this way?

JOHNNY CASH: My daddy left home when I was three, and he didn't leave much to Ma and me, just this old guitar and an empty bottle of booze. Now, I don't blame him cause he run and hid, but the meanest thing that he ever did was before he left, he went and named me "Sue."

WESTLEY: You admit to me that you hide your true identity?

JOHNNY CASH: I made a vow to the moon and stars that I'd search the honky-tonks and bars and kill that man who gave me that awful name.

WESTLEY: You've done nothing but study fighting?

JOHNNY CASH: I was a highwayman. Along the coach roads I did ride with sword and pistol by my side. Many a young maid lost her baubles to my trade. Many a soldier shed his lifeblood on my blade. The bastards hung me in the spring of '25. But I am still alive.

WESTLEY: Have you ever considered piracy? You'd make a wonderful Dread Pirate Roberts.

JOHNNY CASH: I was a sailor. I was born upon the tide and with the sea I did abide. I sailed a schooner round the Horn to Mexico. I went aloft and furled the mainsail in a blow. And when the yards broke off they said that I got killed. But I am living still.

WESTLEY: I myself am often surprised at life's little quirks. I was tormented as a farm boy by true love.

JOHNNY CASH [*snorts in recognition*]: I lie awake at night and wait till she comes in. She stays a little while and then she's gone again. Every question that I ask, I get a lie, lie, lie.

WESTLEY: Where I come from, there are penalties when a woman lies.

JOHNNY CASH: I wonder if she's sorry for leavin' what we'd begun. There's someone for me somewhere, and I still miss someone.

WESTLEY [*nods in agreement*]: True love saved my Buttercup in the Fire Swamp, and she treated it like garbage.

JOHNNY CASH [*cries into his drink*]: Love is a burning thing, and it makes a fiery ring. Bound by wild desire, I fell in to a ring of fire.

WESTLEY: It's not that bad. I'm not saying I'd like to build a summer home there, but the trees are actually quite lovely.

JOHNNY CASH: I keep a close watch on this heart of mine. I keep my eyes wide open all the time.

WESTLEY: Singed a bit, were you?

JOHNNY CASH: I told her, "When your fickle little love gets old, no one will care for you. You'll come back to me for a little love that's true. I'll tell you no and you gonna ask me why, why, why? When I remind you of all of this, you'll cry, cry, cry."

WESTLEY: Life is pain. Anyone who says differently is selling something.

[*the door bangs open, and Agent Kay and Agent Jay—Men in Black—enter*]

AGENT KAY: Johnny?! When did they let you out of jail?

JOHNNY CASH: Far from Folsom prison, that's where I want to stay.

AGENT JAY [*to Westley*]: You know who this guy is?

WESTLEY: I assumed he was no one to be trifled with...

JOHNNY CASH [*to Westley*]: I fly a starship across the Universe divide. And when I reach the other side, I'll find a place to rest my spirit if I can. Perhaps I may become a highwayman again.

AGENT K [*to Johnny Cash*]: You sold a carbonizer with implosion capacity to an unlicensed cephalopod.

Johnny Cash: I always told Billy Joe, "Don't take your guns to town, son." [*sighs*]

Agent K: I want you on the next transport off this rock.

Johnny Cash: Well, I know I had it coming, I know I can't be free.

Westley [*to Kay and Jay*]: Who are you? Are we enemies?

Agent Kay: I'm just a figment of your imagination.

[*Jay grabs Westley and holds him wriggling before Kay*]

Westley [*to the agents*]: I'll beat you both apart! I'll take you both together!

[*Johnny Cash just watches placidly, shaking his head at the unjust roughing-up of Westley*]

Johnny Cash: You wonder why I always dress in black? Well, there's things that never will be right, I know, and things need changin' everywhere you go. But till we start to make a move to make a few things right, you'll never see me wear a suit of white.

Agent K [*to Westley*]: Ever see one of these?

WESTLEY: It's possible. I see a lot of things.

AGENT K: This is called a "neuralyzer." A gift from some friends from out of town. The red eye here isolates and measures the electronic impulses in your brain. More specifically, the ones for memory.

FLASH!

[*Westley stares blankly into space while Kay and Jay hustle Johnny Cash out the door, then slowly comes to*]

WESTLEY: I feel like I've been mostly dead all day... ●

ABOUT THE AUTHOR

"One of online's finest" film critics, or so says trade mag *Variety,*
MaryAnn Johanson is the webmaster and sole critic at Flick
Filosopher [flickfilosopher.com], which debuted in 1997 and is
now one of the most popular movie-related sites on the Internet.
Her blog, Geek Philosophy [geekphilosophy.com], explores the
rise of geek attitudes in popular culture. Johanson is the only
major film critic who is a member of The International Academy of
Digital Arts and Sciences (the Webby organization), an invitation-
only, 500-member body of leading Web experts, business figures,
luminaries, visionaries and creative celebrities. She has appeared
as a cultural commentator on BBC Radio, and she served a judge
at the first Science Fiction, Fantasy and Horror Film Festival at
the 2003 I-Con, the largest SF convention on the East Coast. She
is a founding member of Cinemarati: The Web Alliance for Film
Commentary [cinemarati.org], and is also an award-winning
screenwriter. She lives in New York City. This is her first book.

Printed in the United States
76819LV00003B/169

9 781847 287397